Inquiry in Action

TEACHING COLUMBUS

AVRAM BARLOWE

ANN COOK: SERIES EDITOR

TEACHERS COLLEGE PRESS

COMMUNITY STUDIES, INC

Grateful acknowledgement to the Bill and Melinda Gates Foundation and Community Studies, Inc. for support provided

Distributed by Teachers College Press, 1234 Amsterdam Avenue, New York, NY 10027

ISBN 0-8077-4687-8

Manufactured in the United States of America

11 10 09 08 07 06 05 04   8 7 6 5 4 3 2 1

Contents

Introduction: Inquiry Teaching   5

1. Engaging Students in History   9

2. Debate, Discussion, and Writing   17

3. Teaching Columbus   25

4. Geography and Columbus's Predecessors   48

5, Assignments and Activities: Developing Inquiry Skills   52

6. Final Paper and Conclusion   58

NOTES   63

Introduction

INQUIRY TEACHING

Inquiry teaching views student interest, experience, and viewpoint as the crucial framework for assimilating academic content. Inquiry assumes that the accumulation of information is relatively useless unless learners can articulate and elaborate their own perspectives on the material. In other words, students must be allowed to define and interpret material on their own terms and on the basis of their own experiences.

Inquiry argues that when the opposite occurs, when the teacher dominates definition and interpretation, the student does not thoroughly grasp the material because the exploration of it has already been done for him. The student never takes ownership of the material. The teacher has usurped the student's struggle to make sense of what is being explored by substituting a series of predetermined questions and answers that often bear little resemblance to the student's actual thought process and experience. Inquiry values the individual student's process and experience, not for inherent truth or clarity, but because process and experience together represent the student's way of thinking. Inquiry contends that the learner cannot transcend the limitations of his thought by replacing his thought process with someone else's.

Inquiry teaching insists that development can best occur when an original thought system is expanded. Students begin with their own perspectives and then refine or modify their views through discussion with others. If a student's search for meaning is regarded by a teacher as "wrong," the process is undermined. Instead of predetermined answers, inquiry encourages students to explain things as they see them and then substantiate and expand upon those explanations.

The teacher's role is to initiate activities that help students develop strategies and skills for comprehending and analyzing information, enabling them to speak and write about their unique perspective of the material. Through discussion, debate, interviews with guests, and assigned readings, students are pressed to go beyond comfortable generalizations and substantiate their ideas with evidence. They then collect further information through various forms of research. Together with their classmates, students create and recreate criteria by which they evaluate the often-conflicting perspectives they bring to the classroom.

TRADITIONAL TEACHING

In the overwhelming majority of New York State classrooms, the inquiry approach does not exist. Instead, teachers traditionally rely upon a developmental method. Students are expected to demonstrate mastery of information and concepts as defined by the instructor and in conjunction with city and state curriculum guidelines. The student's viewpoint and analysis of the material are secondary or, at best, implicit. The student is tested for competence in an intentionally limited body of information, and success is measured by the student's ability to reproduce that information.

Teachers seek to elicit students' understanding of the selected information and concepts through developmental lessons, which comprise, in essence, a series of questions designed to evoke predetermined responses. Students then demonstrate mastery when they duplicate the details and concepts in exams and, occasionally, through their writing. Class discussions generally are not part of the assessment process.

A developmental framework is usually accepted even by those seeking to challenge traditional curricula. Retaining the dominant methodology, however, limits the extent to which students are engaged in the study of history, exposed to multiple points of view, committed to meaningful participation in class discussions, and required to use judgment and analysis of evidence to arrive at a conclusion.

AN OPEN-ENDED PROCESS

What follows is an inquiry case study of an American history unit on Columbus. The curriculum provides a detailed example of teaching rooted in multiple perspectives and critical analysis of evidence through discussion and writing. This curriculum is not a blueprint to be copied in the fashion of the traditional lesson plans that educational organizations distribute. Given the open-ended nature of the inquiry process and the role played by students in shaping its curricular focus, the questions, materials, information, and activities of this unit vary each time it is taught. And, while several teaching techniques are discussed, it is crucial that these be seen as part of a larger process in which issues are raised, evidence relating to them is examined, and conclusions are exchanged and debated. It is the understanding of how to guide such a process that is, in my view, central to its effective use.

Avram Barlowe

1   **Engaging Students in History**

ALIENATED STUDENTS

In my experience, the majority of high school students of all backgrounds feel alienated not only from traditional social studies curricula and classrooms, but also from the idea of history itself. For these students, history appears to be irrelevant to their concerns, interests, and feelings. While there are many reasons for this, one contributing factor is that they are consistently denied the chance to express their opinions when exploring historical topics.

The first order of business in my American history classroom is therefore to place student opinions at the center of a discussion. This is a first step in an inquiry that allows students to connect themselves and their values with the history that had previously been an impenetrable abstraction.

ACTIVITY
THE SORT

The vehicle that I use to promote and extend this connection is called a "sort." Generally speaking, sorts are lists or groups of concepts, people, or events that students are asked to order according to a set of criteria they create. To begin a unit on Columbus, for example, students are given a list of prominent figures in America's history (see pages 10–11), with Columbus included alongside 125 others.

Students are asked to read through this list and cross out or ignore any names they do not recognize or know anything about. Next, each student is instructed to select the ten most important figures in American history. Students are encouraged to add people whose names do not appear in the sort if they feel that those individuals should have been included. Then each student is asked to choose the five least important people in American history.

When the lists have been completed, the class is divided into small groups of three to five students. The groups are required to exchange ideas and opinions about their individual lists and reach consensus on a final group list of the six or seven most important figures in American history and the two least important. Each group writes its consensus choices on the chalkboard and appoints a representative to summarize the thinking and discussion that occurred and the criteria the group used.

To begin the larger class discussion, I select one group to present its list and field the questions, comments, or criticisms that the rest of the students may have about the choices or the criteria and procedures used. This process continues until each group has been heard from.

The American History Sort List

Albert Einstein	Elvis Presley	George Bush	Rachel Carson
Edgar Allan Poe	Lee Iacocca	Thomas Jefferson	John D. Rockefeller
Daniel Inouye	W.E.B. DuBois	John Brown	George Washington
Ben Franklin	William H. Taft	Al Capone	Cristobal Columbus
Pontiac	Betsy Ross	Lolita Lebron	Abraham Lincoln
Gabriel Prosser	Paul Revere	Powhatan	William Randolph Hearst
Emma Goldman	Sam Houston	Eugene V. Debs	Elizabeth Cady Stanton
Lucretia Mott	Robert E. Lee	Sequoyah	Benjamin Banneker

Ronald Reagan	Wright Brothers	Harriet Tubman	William Lloyd Garrison
Mary M. Bethune	John F. Kennedy	John Ross	Elijah Muhammad
Crispus Attucks	Harry S. Truman	Henry Clay	Andrew Jackson
Louis Armstrong	Sitting Bull	John Jay	Charlie Parker
M. Luther King, Jr.	Harold Ickes	Jefferson Davis	Joseph McCarthy
James Naismith	Joe Hill	Susan B. Anthony	Anne Hutchinson
Abner Doubleday	Ralph W. Emerson	Woodrow Wilson	Booker T. Washington
J. P. Morgan	Marcus Garvey	Albizu Campos	George Wash. Carver
Malcolm X	I. M. Pei	Daniel Shays	Lyndon B. Johnson
A. Graham Bell	Thomas Paine	Langston Hughes	Douglas McArthur
Berry Gordy	John Adams	Helen Keller	Big Bill Haywood
Ayn Rand	Pocahontas	Mark Twain	Cornelius Vanderbilt
Ella Baker	Patrick Henry	Fannie Lou Hamer	Frederick Douglass
Charlie Chaplin	Jan Matzeliger	Elihu Root	Theodore Roosevelt
Chief Joseph	Denmark Vesey	Cesar Chavez	Thurgood Marshall
Ramon Betances	Babe Ruth	Billie Jean King	J. Robert Oppenheimer
Robert Moses	Samuel Gompers	Sojourner Truth	Walt Whitman
Richard Nixon	Jonas Salk	Rosa Parks	Alexander Hamilton
Henry Ford	James Madison	John L. Lewis	Molly Church Terrell
Margaret Sanger	Thomas Edison	Ida B. Wells	Jean B.P. du Sable
A. Phillip Randolph	Betty Friedan	Jill Johnston	Jesse Jackson
Earl Warren	Paul Robeson	Eleanor Roosevelt	Jeanette Rankin
John Marshall	Lewis & Clark	Marilyn Monroe	Franklin D. Roosevelt
Herman Melville	Richard Wright		

The sort invariably generates a tremendous amount of energy and thinking on the part of the students. As they try to reconcile their choices in their groups and in the general discussions, they express conflicting opinions, raising issues that are vital to both inquiry and learning.

An example of a set of four groups' choices helps to illustrate this:

	Group 1	Group 2	Group 3	Group 4
Most Important	M. Luther King, Jr.	Ben Franklin	M. L. King, Jr.	C. Columbus
	A. Graham Bell	T. Edison	Cesar Chavez	G. Washington
	Albert Einstein	A. Einstein	J.F.Kennedy	Jonas Salk
	Thomas Jefferson	T. Jefferson	Malcolm X	M. L. King, Jr.
	Malcolm X	A. G. Bell	Jesse Jackson	T. Jefferson
	Thomas Edison	M. L. King, Jr.	A. Einstein	Henry Ford
	Thurgood Marshall	Paul Robeson	T. Edison	T. Marshall
Least Important	Johnny Carson	L. Iacocca	Elvis Presley	J. Carson
	Marilyn Monroe	J. Carson	Wyatt Earp	Betsy Ross
	Lee Iacocca	M. Monroe	Billie Jean King	

What constitutes importance in history?

One question that usually emerges as students challenge each other and support or defend their choices is *What constitutes importance in history?* Some argue that an individual should not be selected as important because he or she engaged in "negative" behavior (e.g., "Didn't George Washington own slaves?"). Others claim that scientists and technological innovators are not as central in history as political figures. There is often disagreement about how best to measure an individual's impact on society. There are even instances in which lists are contested because their authors have allegedly showed preferential treatment for persons of certain groups ("Isn't your list saying that black peoples' contributions have been more important than white peoples'?"). Overall, ideas about the meanings of "importance" and "contribution" are debated (sometimes at length, depending on the level of passion and interest provoked), making it increasingly clear that looking at history involves values and points of view.

What Is Your Evidence?

Such debates make students aware that the ability to argue for a particular point of view requires the additional ability to marshal evidence in support of it and that "evidence" is something that must be questioned as well. In the discussion that followed the selection of the most and least important figures mentioned earlier, one student argued that Elvis Presley could not be judged to have had a significant impact on the history of music because he did not write his own material. Others disagreed, claiming it was Elvis's performances that were the more significant measure of his impact. This argument provoked still other students to ask for evidence supporting the charge regarding Elvis's composing role. When challenged, the student who had made the charge was unable to produce such evidence, other than to say that it was "a known fact." While I made the decision not to investigate this issue further, I did explain to the students that we would have to locate and assess more information about Elvis if we wanted to resolve our dispute. Requiring students to research an issue raised and evaluate the supporting pieces of evidence is an essential part of inquiry learning.

PEDAGOGICAL CONCERNS

The sort empowers students to take ownership of the material, a quality all too often absent in classrooms. As opinions, arguments, and information are exchanged, participants are given the opportunity to challenge and learn from one another. They must grapple with differences in their backgrounds insofar as these are expressed through the selections made and points of view articulated.

Teachers unfamiliar with inquiry have often voiced concern that this apparent opening-up of the classroom constitutes an academic land mine replete with intellectual, emotional, and cultural booby traps. Doesn't this approach make a lot of kids feel ignorant? What if a student makes blatantly false claims when offering his point of view? Isn't it the teacher's job to correct him? Aren't you tapping into deeprooted feelings about identity, which can lead to angry, unproductive confrontations? Such questions can best be answered by focusing on the role of the teacher in this activity.

THE TEACHER'S ROLE

My objective in the inquiry process is to provoke questions and ideas about history, in general, and American history, in particular; to facilitate and supervise the exploration of these questions and ideas; to maintain a focus while the exploration occurs; to locate and present evidence from multiple perspectives; and to help students analyze the evidence that our exploration yields or demands.

As teachers develop the techniques associated with inquiry, they learn how to guide the process and engage their students. For example, in the sort described above, I have yet to meet the young person whose possible fear of not knowing names on the list outweighs the desire to make choices about prominent figures in American history and discuss and defend those choices in a small group setting.

Some may object that the sort and other activities centered on the student are based on opinion and not solid information. Certainly, misinformation, all too common in the world at large, is a major concern in any classroom. The question for teachers is not how to suppress it but how best to challenge it. Inquiry teachers attempt to do so by developing learners who subject information to rigorous analysis through discussion and the exchange of views. If patently false information does go unchallenged, the teacher must make a judgment. When the mistake seems to deserve attention, the teacher can ask the erring student to submit supporting evidence to the group. Alternatively, the teacher might choose to present conflicting evidence that would bring the uncontested fallacy into question. As students become more adept at inquiry, they too can challenge misinformation and conduct their own research to present conflicting evidence. In all these instances, students learn to assume responsibility for weighing and evaluating the evidence presented.

No Personal Attacks

The handling of differences around emotionally-charged issues such as race, sex, and class requires a command of the methodology I have been describing. Tense disagreements can arise in inquiry discussions: these must be framed, presented, and reintegrated into the conversation in a calm, clear, and authoritative manner by the teacher. (Here rigorous recording of discussions through note taking is essential since it will help maintain an overall focus. The teacher's support of every student's right to express and develop an opinion is central, with the proviso that no personal attacks can be made on other participants. Students must be able to trust that their teacher will exercise objective judgment and protect their right to be heard. This cannot happen without the teacher's promotion of a commitment to mutual respect ("You can attack a person's ideas, but not the person: you can say, 'your idea is wrong because. . ,' but not 'you're stupid.'").

Of course, what must complement these organizational skills is the teacher's respect for students' experiences and viewpoints. This will require extra time, thought, and effort; the teacher must learn to listen to students' ideas, view them as integral to inquiry, and in turn, use them to guide classroom discussion and activities.

Debate, Discussion, and Writing

Not infrequently, the teacher will feel that student deliberations on a topic have been inadequate—that students lack perspectives that are critical to a broader understanding of the topic under review. Such concerns can be addressed through the creation of a panel on which invited guests debate and exchange ideas about issues the class has been examining.

In the unit on Columbus, I have used a panel consisting of three or four guests who participate in the sort in the same manner as the students have. The panel members present their choices to the class, critique each other's selections, and respond to questions, comments, and criticisms from the students.

Depending on the issues and perspectives the teacher hopes to raise, panel members can be selected who reflect (or willingly pretend to reflect) a particular point of view. In the class whose group decisions are listed on page 18, I selected a high school principal who assumed a progressive role; a veteran of the sixties disguised as a strident conservative; and a member of my school staff who presented a strong populist point of view.

Their choices were as follows:

Most Important		
Progressive	*Conservative*	*Populist*
Thomas Jefferson	G. Washington	The people
F. D. Roosevelt	T. Jefferson	
Samuel Gompers	Abraham Lincoln	
Eugene V. Debs	Henry Ford	
L. B. Johnson	Richard Nixon	
J. F. Kennedy	Ronald Reagan	
Susan B. Anthony		
Rosa Parks		
M. Luther King, Jr.		

Least Important		
The so-called leaders	Elvis Presley	Betsy Ross

Each panelist presented his or her choices with an explanation. A lively exchange among the panelists themselves then followed. The populist panelist who championed "the masses" as the true makers of history charged that both the progressive principal and the hard-line conservative had ignored the role of rank and file action in the creation of change. Offering the sit-ins of the civil rights movement and the petitioning and organized pressure that preceded Jackie Robinson's entry into major league baseball as evidence for his views, the panelist with populist leanings raised an issue that none of the students seemed to have contemplated. The conservative responded to this broadside by arguing that to "romantically elevate 'the people' is to reduce them to faceless automatons as is done in communist, totalitarian societies."

Beyond exposure to new issues and information, what many of the students were witnessing for the first time in a classroom was a thoughtful, reasoned disagreement between adult "experts" on an academic subject. As the students joined in the debate with their responses and questions, they began to experience history as an "argument without end" (see Notes). Their interest and enjoyment were palpable.

The speaker who had made the most traditionally conservative choices was also the most provocative. He was asked why there were no black people on his list. In his response, he drew attention to the prejudice and lack of opportunity black people had faced and concluded that, unfortunately, they had not had a chance to have as important an impact on America's history as had the white men he had selected.

Students responded by confronting him with evidence such as the impact of the civil rights movement and the credit due black inventors. This led to discussions of the relative significance of protest as opposed to legislation, and the civil rights achievements of Lyndon Johnson as opposed to those of Dr. King and Malcolm X. It also took the class back to a point that had been raised previously—namely, the role played by so-called "ordinary people" in shaping events.

The conservative panelist provided the class with exactly the type of challenge hoped for. His agile and fact-filled defense of an unpopular position not only pushed students to articulate ideas, but also convinced some that their arguments were not foolproof and that their evidence was sometimes contrived, confused, or otherwise faulty. When one young man asked why an inventor such as Henry Ford was listed if inventors were not so important, he was quickly told that Ford was not the inventor of the automobile and that, in any case, Ford was listed for his role in advancing the mass production that has contributed so much to the American standard of living. The conservative panelist (who did not reveal his identity until the discussion's end) provided an opportunity for the class to grapple with a position that almost all of them were hostile to, in a manner which would have been much more difficult to maintain had a similar point of view been advanced by one of the students.

The panelists who offered more sympathetic perspectives helped to develop as well as contest many of the arguments the class made. The parts played by leaders and followers in the initiation and construction of popular struggles, social institutions, and cultural trends sparked debate between the principal (the "progressive") and the school staff member (the "populist"), each backed by corresponding groups of students. Here again, the adults and the students exchanged arguments and information.

TEACHER'S ROLE

It is not the inquiry teacher's job in a panel discussion to raise issues or dictate what is being explored. That is the work of the students, who are told at the beginning of the session that it is their responsibility to question and respond to the panelists as well as each other. The teacher serves as moderator, calling on both students and panelists when they wish to speak. However, it is also the teacher's job to maintain an overall focus, soothe frayed tempers, restate arguments so that they can be clearly understood and responded to, and clarify divergent issues so that a clear and comprehensive discussion can occur in which all who wish to express themselves can do so. These duties require sensitivity toward different modes of student expression and thinking, the ability to make impromptu judgments in directing a discussion, and a talent for vigorous note taking so that a written record can be used to review ideas and information.

Inquiry homework assignments depend on the teacher's incorporation of a number of diverse considerations. In developing the assignments, the teacher must take several factors into account: the most critical issues emerging in classroom discussions; the background information required for students to deepen their understanding of the issues; and the reading, writing, research, and analytic thinking skills the teacher wishes to emphasize and cultivate. The teacher must also be knowledgeable about available materials and have some idea of the time required to locate and prepare materials if appropriate ones are not immediately accessible.

The initial homework following the panel debate was based on the notes students had taken during the discussion. They were asked to submit their notes along with a detailed, written response to a panelist's point with which they disagreed and a panelist's point with which they agreed. My purpose here was to reinforce, in intentionally modest terms, the importance of the relationship between argument and evidence.

A second homework underscored this emphasis by asking students to work with more complex and, in most cases, unfamiliar material. Students were asked to read and evaluate selections from *The 100: A Ranking of the Most Influential Persons in History*, by Michael Hart. The Hart book, though limited, presents a clear and thoughtful ranking of individuals whom the author considers most influential. Each selection is accompanied by a two-to-four page defense.

Students were first asked to read Hart's top ten choices, skimming descriptions of persons whose names they did not know. Next, each student was asked to pick one or two of the top ten who did not seem to deserve that ranking. The students were then required to read Hart's explanation for including the "undeserving," writing down the main arguments made on behalf of the individuals in question. Finally, alongside these arguments, the students were to include their own explanations of why they disagreed with Hart's views. The students were also given the option of noting particular statements which they felt needed additional proof.

This homework proved to be very difficult for many in the class. It demanded a level of skill and sophistication that the class was only beginning to develop. Some were uncomfortable or unaccustomed to reading historical material not written in a traditional textbook style. In certain instances, students had problems identifying arguments. Other students were unable to support their disagreements with Hart, which led to frustration and feelings of inadequacy.

Nevertheless, I think the assignment was basically successful. The students enjoyed reading about the people and came up with astute and engaging responses. (One, for example, questioned Hart's selection of Mohammed as history's most influential person on the grounds that Christianity had played a more important role in the triumph of industrialized nations; another argued that the presence of Christ in the top ten was wrong because Christ himself had reached and organized only a small group of people in his lifetime.) While another homework might have provided students with better tools and more information, this one certainly allowed them to wrestle with opinion and information in a new but essentially accessible context.

Another option at this point is an assignment relating to the role played in history by Martin Luther King, Jr., a figure often discussed in the panel debate. Students are given two essays by historians August Meier and Clayborne Carson that disagree on whether Dr. King's involvement was crucial to the success of the civil rights movement (see Notes). The students are asked to respond to this debate by writing papers that include in-depth evaluations of the two views, as well as expressions of their own opinions on the issues. Most students find this assignment relevant and compelling. They spend a good deal of time in class discussing the arguments and critiquing the evidence presented in the articles. They develop examples of their own to explain the material. What proves more difficult, here and throughout the course, is the written analysis of arguments and evidence.

STUDENTS AND WRITING

Student writers can summarize quite clearly the viewpoints and information that Meier and Carson offer, but they have trouble developing their own responses to the historians' arguments and the evidence on which these arguments rest. Students find it very hard to explain why they think a particular contention or supporting piece of information is either convincing or weak. One reason may be the difficulty they have creating as solitary writers the kind of dialogue and debate that exist in an inquiry classroom.

There are times when assignments such as these can be overwhelming, particularly at this early stage of a course. An alternative assignment emerged as we reviewed a videotape of the panel discussion. I first asked students to read Langston Hughes's poem "Let America Be America Again," which stresses the role played by the poor and oppressed "who made America," but whose dream of a just and equal America has yet to be realized. I then required students to write a brief interpretation of the poem's basic message, discussing the responses to the poem that the three adult panelists might have expressed.

Course Overview

Having raised a wide variety of questions about American history and history in general, the course has opened a number of possibilities: It might lean towards research and comparisons of several of the individuals highlighted in the sort and panel discussions. Or it might focus on specific historical events and periods as potential pieces of evidence.

My preference at this point is to investigate the story of Christopher Columbus as the beginning of a unit on European exploration and the conquest of the Americas.

I choose this direction for two reasons. First, Columbus is usually selected, and sometimes debated, during the sort. In some classes, his significance and positive contributions are widely assumed, while in others, students contest his role in fairly sweeping terms. Second, while Columbus certainly does not constitute the beginning of American history, he does represent a gateway to that history, if only because of the way schools traditionally present him. For most Americans, Columbus, more than anyone else they can recall, is the person responsible for this country's origins. Columbus is a common reference point that has been "taught" at an early age to everyone and, as such, is the veritable linchpin upon which so much historical awareness (if it can be called that) is based. Everybody who has been educated in the Western Hemisphere knows something about Columbus.

Four different conceptions of Columbus: *(top left)* a sixteenth century portrait; *(top right)* a painting by Lorenzo Lotto in 1512; *(bottom left)* an engraving from a portrait by Mariano Maella, probably in the late 1700s; *(bottom right)* an engraving from a portrait painted in 1838 by Charles Legrand, whose model was a 1596 engraving.

The Columbus unit begins with a request that students write a brief response to the following: "What do you know and think about Columbus?" or "What do you know about the story of Columbus?" This can be done in class or at home, as long as it is clear that the piece is not to be researched. Students are told they will not be graded for right or wrong answers. Their responses (running two to four pages), which I type with authors' names omitted, are distributed to the class for analysis and discussion. Comments, questions, agreements, and disagreements are solicited and recorded for further investigation.

While there is substantial agreement among students, a look at a few samples reveals more than enough diversity of information to create further points of inquiry.

[STUDENT A] Christopher asked his country for some ships and money and they said no because he wanted to sail west and claimed, with his theory that the earth was round, that he would get there. So he went to Spain, Isabella and Ferdinand gave him three ships and he came to the West Indies looking for the East Indies. Why does he get all the credit?

[Student B] Columbus sailed from the country of Spain and on his voyage discovered America. He thought it was India. He was trying to get to India to trade for spices. His posse consisted of three great ships: the Nina, the Pinta, and the Santa Maria. He went down in history as the man who discovered America.

[STUDENT C] Christopher Columbus never touched North American land—only the West Indies. Sailed in 1492—Nina, Pinta, Santa Maria. Opinion—None, I never met the man.

[STUDENT D] I really don't know about Columbus but I was told that he was an Italian who went to the Spanish to get funding to take a voyage to find East India. However, he really screwed up because he was not the first to land in this hemisphere. In my mind he was probably a person who cared mostly for himself and for stealing the wealth and raw materials from this once great land, though this may or may not be true. The impact I feel is that he made other countries in the world feel that they had the right to take what they wanted just because they wanted to. I believe in God but the Catholic Church had a big part in the atrocities he committed against the Indians.

[STUDENT E] Christopher Columbus asked the king and queen of Spain for money and ships to set sail to India. The Nina, the Pinta, and Santa Maria sailed to what they thought was India but in actuality was America. Columbus named the natives Indians. Year: 1492. I personally think that Christopher Columbus's part in history is a bunch of hype and his voyage to America is misinterpreted as him discovering America. I am pretty sure that others found America before Columbus. My knowledge of him is pretty spotty due to the fact that I never really had a good history class. The facts that I do know are an accumulation of bits and pieces picked up throughout school.

[STUDENT F] All I know about Christopher Columbus is that he discovered America, that he worked for the King and Queen of Spain, and that he was white and sailed in a small boat.

[Student G] Christopher Columbus was an Italian from I think either Bologna or Venice, or Florence, and he wanted to find a new trade route to India. He asked Queen Isabella three or four times before she gave him the money. I have even heard he might have had an affair with her. He was given three ships, as we all know—the Nina, the Pinta, and the Santa Maria. He reached what he believed to be India in the year 1492 A.D. He laid a claim on it for Spain and then returned to Spain, presented everything and after that I'm not sure.

[STUDENT H] Christopher Columbus was the Father of America. He was the first man to come across the water in little boats. He discovered the U.S.A.

[STUDENT I] Christopher Columbus and all the other people in those days thought that when you went far out into the ocean, there was a big drop-off, and they were always too afraid to check it out. They also thought that there were sea monsters. Columbus also tried to find a new route to India and the Orient! But like a fool he went the wrong way and found Cuba, South America and later on went to America. But before his mission he had trouble getting a crew, money, and a ship. Finally, the queen of Spain gave him some money. During the mission, many of his men went crazy. Some tried to go for a mutiny. I think he's a fake. The Vikings found America first. Columbus killed innocent people. I got this info from my fourth grade teacher.

[STUDENT J] Cristobal was an Italian. He was a navigator at the service of Spain. In trying to find a new way to get to India, he accidentally discovered a new land. It wasn't until he died that the land he believed was India was recognized to be not India but a new land, a new continent. He believed, unlike many others in his time, that the earth was round.

[STUDENT K] Christopher Columbus sailed across the ocean and discovered America (even though the Indians were already here). He was the one who discovered that the world was round, not flat. He had several ships like the Pinta, the Santa Maria, and Nina.

[Student L] Christopher Columbus was a Portuguese sailor who wanted to find a water route to the Indies, which were a source of spices that could not be found in Europe. After being turned down by the King and Queen of Portugal, Queen Isabella of Spain financed his first voyage in 1492. His three ships were the Nina, the Pinta, and the Santa Maria. Most of his sailors were criminals from Spain. Columbus faced scurvy and mutiny on the voyage across the ocean. After he landed in the New World, he met some people he dubbed Indians, assuming it was India. He made three more trips to the New World.

It is relatively easy to clarify certain aspects of the information appearing in these selections (e.g., "He discovered the U.S.A."). Other discrepancies merit deeper class research. Within an inquiry class, determining which issues deserve the greatest attention is guided in part by student interest and in part by the teacher, who must consider student needs, personal resources, and historic import.

QUESTIONING

Listed below are a number of questions explicitly and implicitly raised during a discussion of the "What do you know about Columbus?" essays, which were typed and distributed to one class:

1. How responsible was the Catholic Church for the murder of American Indians?

2. What was Columbus's nationality or ethnic group?

3. How did he die?

4. Did he die from syphilis?

5. Was Columbus the only one who knew that the world was round, or did other people know it?

6. Is Columbus given credit for what was basically an accident?

7. Why is there a school holiday for Columbus in the eastern U.S.A. and not in the western U.S.A.?

8. Should there be holidays for groups or for average people instead of for leaders and heroes?

9. What should the word "discover" mean?

10. Is it right to say that someone "discovered" a place in which there were already people?

11. How long was his trip? (five months? six months? a year? two?)

12. Was he lost, or did he purposely find the West Indies?

13. What was Columbus's exact route? Where exactly did he land?

14. Did Columbus land on any continents?

15. How did the Europeans get to India before Columbus?

16. How did the Native American people get to North and South America?

17. What was Columbus's motive for sailing here in the first place?

18. What exactly happened when Columbus arrived in the New World?

19. Is Columbus responsible for slavery in America?

20. Did slavery exist before it happened in America? If so, for how long?

21. Did Columbus start large-scale killing and robbery of other people in world history?

22. If Columbus did bad things, wouldn't any other explorer have done the same?
23. How many people did Columbus kill and how many of his crew were killed?
24. What would America be like today if Columbus's voyage had not taken place?
25. Did Columbus die in prison?

This list, while drawn from one specific class, is fairly representative. Though some may maintain that the students' lack of knowledge precludes learning in an inquiry setting, I have found that investigating even the most basic concepts and questions is highly productive. Teachers need to resist interjecting their own questions at this point and accept, perhaps on faith, that the broader issues, if not immediately raised, will certainly emerge as inquiry proceeds, particularly if appropriate resources are brought to bear.

RESEARCH
AN INTRODUCTION TO HISTORIOGRAPHY

Having established a few essential questions, the class is now in a position to conduct some basic research. However, inexperience in collecting and analyzing historical information is common among almost all students taking this course. I have therefore devised an activity to introduce students to new sources of information while encouraging them to continue the process of forming opinions and evaluating evidence.

I divide the class into small groups of four and distribute four or five readings about the Columbus story to each group. Using each source, the students are required to pick out (and, in some cases, underline) evidence relating to questions raised in class; students are asked to select the reading which they regard as the best source of information on Columbus himself, his voyages, and the consequences of his voyages. Members of each group are then encouraged to come to a consensus.

Such activity is complex and will often require several class sessions. Some teachers may be inclined to assign the readings (running as much as four or five pages each) as homework. I prefer to use class time because much of the material and many of the required tasks are unfamiliar to students, as is the focus I wish to emphasize; monitoring the way students approach the work is therefore essential.

The Reading Selections

Over the years, I have collected a wide variety of accounts of Columbus and his exploits. For this assignment, I often select:

A one-page excerpt from a 1963 junior high school textbook published by the Singer Corporation (*This Is Our Land*) that hails Columbus as a hero and mentions in passing that Indians sold gold ornaments to him and were "brought" to Europe in order to prove that he had reached America.

A somewhat lengthier reading from an American history textbook used by traditional NYC public high schools.

Two pages from Samuel Eliot Morison's Pulitzer Prize-winning biography of Columbus—*Christopher Columbus, Mariner*—in which Morison stresses the intelligence and bravery of Columbus and, acknowledging Columbus's "flaws and defects," insists that it was "largely the defects which made him great—his strong will, his superb faith in God and in his own mission as the Christ-bearer to lands beyond the sea."

Howard Zinn's virtual indictment of Columbus, a man he views as guilty of genocide, in a piece excerpted from *A People's History of the United States*.

Part of a beautifully illustrated Italian children's book, *The Travels of Columbus*, which paints a detailed but essentially romantic portrait of his explorations.

Students are generally able to handle these readings but, as many teachers know, a reading that is too difficult can cause frustration, especially in students unaccustomed to reading analytic source materials. I may therefore adapt or re-write a selection in order to increase accessibility. (For this particular exercise, I have adapted a few versions, on varying levels of difficulty, of both the Zinn and Morison selections.) Care must be taken, however, to remain faithful to the arguments and evidence presented in a work that is being streamlined and paraphrased.

A dilemma may arise when students of different skill levels use different versions of the same reading. The problem has largely to do with how students feel about using sources they perceive as either easier or more demanding than those used by fellow classmates. Generally speaking, my experience has been that when this issue is dealt with in a straightforward manner, students experience far less anxiety about academic skill gaps than do the adults who are teaching them, especially when they have already experienced their ability to participate fully with each other in classroom discussions. This is not to suggest, however, that skill development be ignored. Teachers often neglect the more specific proficiencies that are essential to the development of larger skills. Analytic reading and writing, for example, are given short shrift by teachers who rely solely on assignments, grades, and brief comments to improve student performance.

Teachers may need to create various tutorial contexts (beyond the classroom) to tackle academic weaknesses existing to varying degrees in almost every student. These more individualized contexts are as vital for student development as classroom activity. To help students overcome their deficiencies, it is important for teachers to observe how students understand, react to, and work on assignments, and in this regard, the more direct the dialogue between students and teachers, the better.

The discussions that follow the reading assignments often focus upon the evidence related to specific questions raised by students. The class may also engage in debates concerning the reliability of sources. As the discussion progresses, the teacher's role is to maintain the focus, record the issues raised, highlight points that seem to have been resolved, and summarize disagreements deserving of further inquiry. These range from seemingly tangential questions to exchanges regarding the nature and ethics of Columbus's voyages in the overall context of European exploration.

PRIMARY SOURCES

Analysis of readings sometimes leads to sharp divisions among the students. In one class, a student argued that Columbus's treatment of Native Americans was possibly justified. He was able to convince some of his fellow students that we needed more information before we could condemn the explorer. I seized on his point and decided to focus the class's attention on a further selection of primary sources. Following a quick search, I selected three readings to present to students the following day. The assignment, based on these readings, follows:

In yesterday's class, we spent a good deal of time debating Columbus's role in American history. A key question came up during our discussion: Was Columbus somehow justified in his treatment of the Indians?

To answer this question, we decided that we first needed information on two other questions:

1. What was Indian life like before Columbus arrived?
2. How did the Indians greet, treat, and respond to Columbus when he arrived?

To help you explore these questions, I have provided you with three different sources of information:

A) Columbus's "Letter to King Ferdinand and Queen Isabella on His First Voyage."
B) Excerpts from *The History of the Indies* by Bartolome Las Casas, a Spanish priest who participated in the conquest of Cuba and became a severe critic of Columbus and Spanish policy.
C) Excerpts from the writings of a Spanish monk who attacked Las Casas's work and supported Spanish treatment of the Indians (see Notes).

Read through each selection and underline evidence you find that helps to answer our questions. Be prepared to submit this evidence to the class for discussion and analysis.

Homework: Use the research you have conducted in this assignment along with your memory of today's discussion to write a short

The Spaniards hanging Indians and setting fire to their houses. Engraving by Bartolome de las Casas.

essay (of no less than two pages) that answers either question one or question two.

The assignment generated activity lasting several days. The students enjoyed working with primary sources, and a host of evidence was offered, compared, and debated. Once again, the discussion lasted longer than the single session I had anticipated. The students explored issues such as the nature of Mayan human sacrifice, the communal lifestyle of Taino and Arawak Indians, and the implications of the conflict that existed among different indigenous peoples.

Discussions also included comparisons of European and Indian lifestyles.

PEDAGOGICAL CONCERNS The written work that followed these discussions was, in most cases, somewhat less inspired than the classroom exchanges. As writers, the students experienced difficulty in elaborating upon their ideas and responding to arguments they disagreed with, perhaps because the struggle to construct and follow an outline distracted them. However, all of the homeworks unquestionably benefited from the discussions that preceded them. In my view, this is because inquiry stresses the organization of arguments as well as the presentation of substantiating evidence. It thus helps young writers to understand that non-fiction writing is essentially the organized expression of ideas (in this case, the ideas debated in the classroom).

Typically, as the Columbus inquiry proceeds, the minor factual questions are resolved. Larger questions, however, are often more difficult to settle. Here, it is very important for the teacher to carefully delineate what the disagreements are so they may be clearly understood. Sometimes, even misinformation can provide fruitful learning opportunities for students.

I offer one such example. Several years ago, in a different school setting, I used Columbus's first letter to Ferdinand and Isabella. As we read aloud what was for most of the students a very lengthy document, one young man decided that Columbus's statement that the Indians "are still of the opinion that I come from the sky, in spite of all the intercourse they have had with me," was essentially a confession of rape. He submitted this opinion and evidence to the class and received overwhelming support. To me, it seemed clear that Columbus was referring to social rather than sexual intercourse, but instead of correcting or arguing with the students, who were quite proud of their apparent discovery, I suggested that we pursue the matter further so as to be absolutely certain.

Someone suggested that we look up the word "intercourse" in the dictionary. We did, and, of course, found that the word had two basic definitions. Which one, then, had Columbus been using? The consensus that had existed began to dissipate as the second meaning became known and as the larger text from which the sentence containing the word had been extracted was reread. Many, however, were still convinced that they had the goods on Columbus.

A diverse panel of adult outsiders was brought in to examine the evidence in question. Students presented a summary of the work they had been doing and an explanation of the controversy that had emerged about the meaning of "intercourse." The panelists, while agreeing that rape had probably been a part of Columbus's crew's exploits, were unanimous in their view that the evidence students had presented was "questionable," at best. Dialogue with these adults seemed finally to convince most of the class that they had been wrong. They nevertheless felt quite satisfied with the inquiry because they had enjoyed testing their hypothesis and having their views taken seriously.

ACTIVITY
CONDUCTING INTERVIEWS

One subject that consistently emerges in student discussions regards traditional high school textbooks' omission of information about the enslavement, murder, and robbery of the Indians "discovered" by Columbus. Many students are surprised to learn that the explorer was involved in such activities, and they become angry when they examine the textbooks and discover no mention of this. One class was so irritated by this omission that I invited a senior member of a high school social studies department to discuss the text selected for use in his high school. I wanted to offer students a chance to develop their position and work with concrete historical evidence as they argued their ideas.

I explained the class's focus to this teacher and provided him with the source materials we had been using. I did not explore his personal perspective on the teaching of history. The teacher reviewed the material and came to the class prepared to answer students' questions. The session lasted about an hour and the excerpts below provide a record of how the students handled their assignment. The excerpts are taken from a transcript based on my notes, which the students received and analyzed the following day.

TAMU: Do you agree with the stuff that is written in the book, the textbook they use in your school?

TEACHER: Well, I just re-read it last night . . . It's an innocuous, non-controversial reading. Most high school texts nowadays are mush, an unappetizing bowl of oatmeal . . . There's not a hell of a lot in it. The texts are not essentially for education; they exist mainly for political reasons, which is to say that parents expect texts and will call up the school when they see their child does not have a textbook. Parents never complain about the content or what's in the book, just about not having it. Again, any teacher worth their salt will go out and find other sources to use alongside of any text.

SEQUOYAH: How do you personally feel about Columbus?

TEACHER: Well, I base my thinking about him mainly on the two sources I have read. One of these is the two-volume work of Samuel Eliot Morison, *Admiral of the Ocean Sea*. What I get from Morison, whom I trust, is that Columbus was an extraordinary seaman. A lesser seaman would not have been able to accomplish what he did. He was not a particularly nice guy, and he was avaricious and rather greedy, but this was not out of keeping with the tenor of the times. However, his greed had a direction as he attempted to look out for his brothers. . . .

Columbus was very abusive of the Indians, he didn't care much about them, and he was probably a thief. Columbus's map was the ace in the hole that he needed to get the Queen's council of advisors' approval of his voyage. But he couldn't produce it on request, probably because he or one of his brothers stole it from the files of Portugal's King John, for whom they had worked. Also, on his voyage, he posted a twenty-four-hour-a-day lookout for land, promising a reward (a sum of gold) to whoever was the first to see it. Columbus not only failed to pay his debt to the man who saw land first, but he claimed the honor and the money for himself.

TAMU: How would the historians know this information, like the stuff about the map?

DAN: And why do you believe what a historian like Morison has to say?

TEACHER: Morison is an extremely knowledgeable historian when it comes to exploration, and particularly navigation. I remember reading things he had to say about Sir Francis Drake's voyages around the West Coast, near what is now California. My own sea trips off that coast confirmed everything that he had written.

DAN: Did you read anything in Morison's book about Columbus being a mass murderer? Based on what we have read of his, I don't think Morison would be likely to use that word.

TAMU: What is your gut personal feeling about Columbus?

TEACHER: My gut personal feeling is not what counts. Columbus was a great seaman, not a great humanitarian. But his main purpose was to act as a seaman, to explore the unknown and it's on that basis that I judge him.

JULIAN: Do you think that Columbus opened the New World to slavery, atrocities, and the abuse and exploitation of others?

TEACHER: I think that the subsequent extermination of the native population in Mexico was mainly the result of Spanish policy, and you can't blame an individual person for this.

JULIAN: But when they returned home as heroes, whether they lied or not about how much gold there was, everyone else in Europe jumped on the bandwagon. If Columbus hadn't done that . . .

TEACHER: What I'm saying is that it was Spanish policy that was responsible. The things you are talking about would've happened because of Spanish policy. In the northern hemisphere, which is now the United States, the British gave land grants to individuals or companies. So the land that was given to William Penn became Pennsylvania. Under the Spanish kings, land was never given away. It was given to people for use, but after twenty years, it reverted to the crown. Now, if you know that something is yours forever, what will you do with it?

JULIAN: Take care of it, but . . .

TEACHER: Now, if you know that you are only going to have land for twenty years or so, what will you do with it?

JULIAN: Make my money and get out.

TEACHER: Yes, and it was that policy that led to many of the atrocities.

JULIAN: But even up here, it was still the same thing, the same result. Europeans were after raw materials that belonged to the people who lived here, and they took them by force. So, in a sense, it's the same thing.

TEACHER: I hear you.

LIZ: You said it was Spanish policy that led to slavery?

TEACHER: Yes.

LIZ: Don't you think the desire for gold also had something to do with this?

TAMU: I agree with Julian to a point. Something would have happened in this way, even if Columbus had never come here. But I think you're putting a pillow under the fall here, you're cushioning or blanketing mass murder by saying it was a policy and not people that was involved.

DAN: Would you agree that two-hundred-and-fifty-thousand people died within a short time after Columbus arrived? I think it is Zinn who says that.

TEACHER: Yes, I accept Zinn as a reliable source.

DAN: Well, Zinn also says that in Morison's work, which I believe is two volumes, there is only one paragraph which deals with this fact, this issue. . .

TAMU: Yeah, you have to understand where this man's mind is at. Your good friend Columbus wasn't bothered in the least at the death of these people.

LIZ: You said that you trust Morison's judgment. How does his lack of mention or discussion of Indian genocide influence your opinion of his overall treatment of Columbus?

TEACHER: You have to understand that historians deal with different aspects of history. Zinn and Morison are dealing with different aspects. Morison is more concerned with the voyages. As far as personal judgments are concerned, I'm not sure I can make them.

YOKO: Why not?

TEACHER: If 250,000 or more Indians died, we have to ask who and what was the cause of that. I think it was more the result of Spanish policy . . . so it may not be an individual. . .

DANIELLE: I think that Columbus had no good points. He was trying to increase trade and instead he bumped into a continent which he thought was something that it wasn't. If he had stayed in Europe, on the other side of the Atlantic, there would have been no mass murder, no slavery, and the native people might have had the chance to develop in their own time and in their own way.

DAN: I want to come back to the text you were asked to look at, the one they use in your high school. Whether it's supposed to be controversial or not, don't you think there should be some mention of the fact that mass murder took place in the islands claimed by Columbus? Instead, it's completely left out, and it's an important fact. Omitting it is a way of justifying it, don't you think?

LIZ: Do you think that someone who has done what Columbus has done deserves to have a holiday?

SHONTANU: Or a parade where -

TEACHER: Let me answer that by telling you what they do in South America and Central America. They celebrate El Dia de la Raza, which means "the day of the race." They celebrate the day a new race was born in the world, which is what I think we should do. They acknowledge the intermingling of whites, blacks, and Indians. . . In the midst of all this death and slaughter, there was a life side to all this.

Now, as for the textbook issue, I agree with you one hundred percent. The reason for it is that that's the way it is, right or wrong. It is that way because in order to make a profit, that's what certain textbook companies have to do. The textbooks have to be approved in certain southern states each year, like in Tennessee or Texas. The publishers have to go down to these southern states, where the book is approved or not approved by very conservative people. If it is passed for approval there, it is usually okay for use throughout the country.

In order to pass this approval, this is what they do. Texts are not produced for more liberal, sophisticated markets like the one we have in New York City. That's the way it is. They say, "Well, we've got to make a dollar."

In the analysis of these exchanges, which took place when the class reviewed the transcript, the students debated a number of issues. These included:

1. The relationship of the individual to the society he serves.
2. The extent to which the difference between Zinn and Morison was the result of difference in focus versus difference in attitude.
3. The degree to which the teacher's argument about why textbooks omitted Columbus's genocidal actions was true or false, and whether or not the teacher's analysis in general was a rationalization of some sort.

The teacher was invited back and questioned further, particularly concerning the last two points. This led to a student-generated discussion of Eurocentrism in the curriculum, what could be done about it, and how the teacher approached Columbus in his classroom. The teacher responded that the students' use of comparative sources had impressed him a great deal and that he would attempt to incorporate this method in his teaching.

PEDAGOGICAL CONCERNS

What struck me about my students' interaction with this teacher was their ability to engage him quite effectively in a general argument, while they failed to use much of the specific factual information contained in the readings to make their case.

Students preferred to poke holes in the teacher's fact-based conclusions and then advance their own extensive grievances. The exchange between the teacher and Julian about Columbus and Spanish colonial policy is a good example of this. In some cases, such as in their criticism of Morison's trivialization of genocide, students were more thorough, but generally they chose to build logical constructs with the material that the teacher selected.

I raised this observation with them after the second session, using the printed transcript to illustrate my point. They conceded the truth of my observation, but maintained that what I was asking them to do was not an easy thing and that they needed more experience. While I agree that lack of experience was certainly an issue, I also feel that the tendency to neglect evidence gleaned from research underscores one of the significant challenges in inquiry teaching.

I had succeeded in encouraging students to "find their own voices," but they needed to be pushed beyond simply generating their own arguments to making well-reasoned defenses of those arguments. Students need opportunities to expand their analytic abilities by seeking out and using relevant evidence. The cultivation of intellectual curiosity and discipline can inform passionate belief and, in my view, makes an important contribution to the development of democratic decision-making and critical activism.

Geography and Columbus's Predecessors

An understanding of the relevant geography must underlie any examination of Columbus. Students must gain exposure to those individuals and peoples who voyaged across the Atlantic before Columbus and the various disputes surrounding their efforts. Basic geography, like the exploration accounts, can be approached from an inquiry perspective.

Students familiar with social and political concerns relating to Columbus's travels are usually quite curious to review his itinerary or, in many cases, to examine it for the first time. When they are grouped and asked to identify on blank maps the routes, destinations, and landing sites of Columbus as well as other explorers, they approach this task seriously. When stymied, they quite willingly use atlases to obtain information.

READINGS AND DISCUSSION

I often begin a look at Columbus's transatlantic predecessors by using material from Ivan van Sertima's *They Came Before Columbus*. I present the students with photographs of Olmec stone heads taken from this book, and I ask them to speculate on where and when these heads might have been made. Many observe the African features in the faces of the heads; invariably, some claim that they were made in Africa. I then reveal to them that, in fact, the heads were created in Mexico and that, according to the author from whose book the pictures are taken, they were constructed by African voyagers well before Columbus's arrival. The question of whether and how Africans might have come to the Western Hemisphere before Columbus is thus raised and debated.

Black warrior dynasts in ancient Mexico. (*left*) Olmec Negroid stone head (San Lorenzo V). *(right)* Olmec Negroid stone head (San Lorenzo IV).

Olmec Negroid stone head (Tres Zapotes II).

Students then proceed to an examination of van Sertima's additional evidence supporting this claim. I distribute ten-page packets of captioned visual material gleaned from his book. Each page contains an illustration, map, or photograph which the students are asked to critique as evidence. As students explore why they accept or reject the "proof" offered on each page, they raise questions requiring further research.

For example, a photograph of Heyerdahl's Ra II, accompanied by a brief explanation of how its construction and rudderless voyage were similar to those of pre-Columbian Africans, has in the past prompted the following inquiries:

Where exactly did Heyerdahl sail from?

Did he use a compass?

What kind of supplies did his crew take?

Did the African boatmen from Lake Chad who built the boat use any modern equipment while building it?

Were the currents in the Atlantic Ocean the same several hundred years ago as they are today?

Was Heyerdahl's re-enactment unfair or unreal because he (unlike the Africans or Columbus) actually knew where he was heading?

These questions become tools which the students use as they turn to the text itself in search of further information and explanation. I facilitate this process by selecting the two or three pieces of visual evidence arousing the sharpest interest. I locate the corresponding pages in van Sertima, and present them to the students, section by section, for discussion. This does not expose them to the full breadth of his argument, which can only be absorbed by reading the entire book. It does, however, introduce them to sophisticated historical research and polemic, something that any empowered high school student can appreciate, if not fully digest.

Once again, a host of accompanying readings and activities can enhance such a unit. As a follow-up to the selective reading and analysis of *They Came Before Columbus*, two adults who have read van Sertima's book might engage in a debate over the validity of van Sertima's thesis. Observation of this debate would partially compensate for students' inexperience with scholarly papers. In addition, there is a substantial body of non- scholarly material that examines the various claims made on behalf of those who allegedly arrived before Columbus and his fleet. An examination of these sources invariably highlights the major difference between Columbus and his predecessors, in that conquest and colonization did not seem to be among the aims of the earlier explorers. Students may speculate why that was so.

Assignments and Activities:
Developing Inquiry Skills

An assortment of written homeworks helps to further reinforce and expand student comprehension. Many of these assignments require that students complete a reading, analyze its content, and develop a personal response to it. The readings and corresponding questions vary in difficulty. Some are readily answered by nearly all students, while others require greater intervention and support on the part of the teacher. The basic demand that the student use evidence to articulate a point of view is constant, however. When a particular assignment yields an especially interesting set of responses, logic dictates that these be brought to the class as a whole for further analysis.

INTRODUCTORY ASSIGNMENTS

One of the more accessible assignments I have given in recent years presents students with two articles (and corresponding photographs) that describe contrasting Columbus Day activities. The first article covers the various participants in a New York Columbus Day parade. The second reports on a "Day of Mourning" protest march conducted by Indians in the Central American city of San Salvador on the same day (see Notes).

Students are asked to read both short articles, describe what they think are the basic differences between the two commemorations, and explain why they think the differences exist. They are also asked to discuss whether it is fair to say that one of the parades is a more appropriate way to remember Columbus than the other, and to express and explain personal preferences, if they have them.

Another introductory-level assignment requires a response to a relatively short but fact- and argument-filled single document, such as a letter to the editor, an editorial from a newspaper, or an Op-Ed piece from *The New York Times*. A somewhat more exacting version takes the students back to Michael Hart's defense of Columbus as the ninth most influential person in the history of the world, and asks students for a fairly detailed critique of the defense.

ADVANCED ASSIGNMENTS   A different kind of challenge is provided by assignments that require students to react to the more scholarly attacks upon and defenses of Columbus, which have appeared in the media and in recent historical analyses. For example, I might assign students to analyze two reviews of Kirkpatrick Sale's new book on Columbus, *The Conquest of Paradise,* which is a fairly strong indictment of the explorer and of European conquest in general. The review, written by syndicated columnist Lawrence Hall, is admiringly sympathetic. The other review, by historian William McNeil, is essentially negative (see Notes). This assignment proves quite challenging, and much of the work accompanying it is done in the classroom, where I can support student efforts.

Classroom support is also critical when students are asked to respond to scholarly articles, such as one by Basil Davidson, in which he makes the argument that racism as we experience it today is the direct legacy of Columbus's voyages (see Notes). The benefits of reading even difficult academic papers are enormous, as students bring rich and varying interpretations to the evaluation of the ideas of writers of Davidson's caliber.

A homework that pushes students to apply what they have learned

about Columbus and, at the same time, develop a more critical understanding of how younger children learn about the explorer requires student analysis of a chapter from a children's book about Columbus. Armstrong Perry's *The Voyages of Christopher Columbus* is a fairly detailed book, nearly two hundred pages in length, which was written for twelve- or thirteen-year-olds. It combines fictional quotations with selections from Columbus's journal. The passages depict Columbus as a noble, patriotic gentleman-entrepreneur, full of paternalistic concern for the primitive Indians he encounters.

Students who attempt a thorough critique of this book are given a choice of preparing a paper or an outline for a paper. The outline option equips students with a structure that allows them to hunt through the text, gathering the evidence needed to advance their particular points of view. To those who feel this is perhaps too ambitious a task for their students to complete individually, I would again suggest that any of these assignments might be adapted for use inside the classroom itself.

Depending on the level of student interest and the availability of resources, a class can continue to explore Columbus in a number of enriching contexts. Students can visit other classrooms or examine and critique other classes' work in this area. It is especially useful for students to observe and question elementary school children who are first learning about Columbus. This experience will give high school students insight into how education works and how ideology is perpetuated; they can identify easily with younger children and, at the same time, contemplate a larger informational context.

It is also helpful to have students design various quizzes, lesson plans, and topic outlines for the teaching of Columbus in the high school classroom. In one class, for example, I divided the students into three groups and asked each group to develop a list of at least ten questions that a student possessing "a good understanding" of Columbus's activities should be able to answer.

The following three lists were produced:

Group 1

1. Where did Columbus land?
2. What tribes did Columbus and his men meet?
3. How, according to Columbus's letters and journals, was he treated?
4. How did Columbus treat the Indians?
5. How many Indians did he kill?
6. What are three things that Bartolomeo de las Casas accused Columbus of?
7. Name one instance in which Columbus lied to the royalty he served.
8. What part of the American mainland did Columbus visit?

9. What were the dates of Columbus's voyages?
10. What were the most important discoveries made by Columbus and why were they important?

Group 2

1. How did Columbus change the way of life of the Indians he met?
2. Why was the European mentality so barbaric in dealing with the Indians when Europe was supposed to be the more civilized society?
3. The men whom Columbus left behind when he returned to Spain were so irresponsible that they had to use force to control the Indians. Why?
4. Did Columbus have a bad effect on the Indians? Give examples.
5. Did Columbus modernize America? If so, in what aspects? If not, did he do anything detrimental?
6. Was Columbus right to destroy the Indian way of life to make expansion for the Europeans possible?
7. What records of what happened are most believable? Why?
8. Do you think Columbus's cruelty towards the Indians should be taught in school? Why or why not?
9. Do you think Columbus should be held personally responsible for the cruelty to the Indians?

Group 3

1. When, if ever, did Columbus set foot on America?
2. When was Columbus's first voyage?
3. Why did Columbus come to America?
4. When he got here, what country did Columbus think he was in?

5. How many people were on each of his ships?
6. How did the natives greet Columbus and his crew?
7. How did Columbus's men test their weaponry when they got to the New World?
8. How many natives were killed between 1492 and 1508?
9. Did Columbus enslave the natives?
10. What kind of religion and way of life did the natives have?

Each of the three sets of questions had a slightly different focus and each contained different strengths and weaknesses.

I felt that a focused critique of each list could promote an even stronger grasp of the issues implicit in the Columbus debate as well as of the factual information in which that debate is rooted. I distributed copies of the lists to each student and then, for homework, asked them to select the "three best" and "three worst" questions appearing on any of the lists. The students were to write up an explanation for each of their choices, and to prepare a rough compilation of eight final questions that a student with a good understanding of Columbus should be able to answer.

These homework assignments were used in our next few classes to evaluate and prepare a single list of questions that might be used to test for a "good understanding" of the Columbus material. Student creation of this "quiz" provided a forum for broad-scale analysis of the overarching themes of the class's study of Columbus.

6   Final Paper and Conclusion

The assignment that culminates the Columbus unit is a two-part paper that asks students to retell the story of Columbus and evaluate whether he deserves to be recognized as an American hero. The first part of the paper, which most students relish, requires them to integrate new-found information and opinion into a familiar outline. The second part demands a thorough discussion of arguments on both sides of the hero question, as well as a weighing of those arguments. In a concluding section, students are asked to develop their personal opinions.

Despite the preparation and skill-building of the previous home-works and classroom activities, the writing of the second part is not a simple task. In undertaking it, students experience a variety of difficulties. It is not easy for them to organize their ideas, develop their arguments beyond glib generalizations, articulate and analyze the arguments they disagree with, or locate and integrate appropriate supporting information.

There are a number of methods that can be employed to help students negotiate these difficulties. Each method requires a great deal of teacher time and effort. In an American history class I team-taught several years ago, a colleague and I assisted our class in a collective writing process. I would stand at the blackboard in the front of the room, writing and rewriting, as my colleague fielded student ideas and sentences; we thus coordinated the class's editorial suggestions. Each day, a different student would copy whatever had gone up on the board, and after two weeks, a class paper on Columbus emerged. This paper was then submitted to a teacher panel for comments and criticisms.

FINAL DEBATE

It is often useful to parallel independent paper writing with a debate between two adult panelists regarding Columbus's hero status. Listening to panelists' exchanges and questioning panelists' arguments helps the students grasp the parameters of the debate and flesh out their own views. The debate should be followed by a homework that asks students to use their notes to recapitulate and respond to points made by the panelists. The debate may also be followed by an activity in which students search for pro and con arguments embedded in a series of newspaper columns that address the issue.

WRITING THE FINAL PAPER

I currently prefer to preface the writing of the paper with an exercise requiring students to think about the possible cases that could be made for or against Columbus's heroism. I ask them to write down all the ideas, arguments, and evidence that come to mind, and to draft an outline that presents these in an organized form. I examine each outline, jot down suggestions, meet with individual students where it seems appropriate, return the work, and ask for a second draft of the outline. When this has been submitted, the students begin to write a first draft of the paper.

In most cases, these papers require the kind of rewriting that necessitates supportive but demanding one-on-one, student-teacher conferences. My criticism during these sessions is directed at the students' ability to focus, organize and support their ideas on paper (i.e., to advocate effectively for their basic position). As always, I ask that they respond as specifically as possible to evidence (e.g., How many Indians died from disease? Do these numbers absolve Columbus?). I often press them into further research when they cannot make their cases. I may probe and politely challenge views I personally disagree with, but I will not "correct" them, in a traditional sense. If exposure to a multiplicity of perspectives has not already had some effect, the imposition of my views in this context is not likely to teach young people very much, other than that their teacher has the capacity to overwhelm their arguments.

Some might claim that the average teacher does not have the time to provide each student with this kind of individual conference. To this, I can only argue that, for me, such attention is critical and the best way I have found to help students understand the link between the analytical exchanges of the classroom and the writing skills we are asking of them. If neither traditional nor alternative schools can accommodate such one-on-one exchanges, they are denying young people the full array of skills they will need to further themselves in the world.

CONCLUSION
THE INQUIRY MODEL

I have attempted to show in this exposition of inquiry teaching that the open-ended, intellectually provocative, and rigorous curriculum I am trying to develop is an important part of the inquiry approach to education. Such a curriculum is not, as critics would have it, a stacked deck intent on indoctrinating its students. It serves rather to open up conventional approaches to the teaching of history that, whatever their strengths, cannot suffice in explaining and changing the world as we know it.

There is no denying that a progressive political perspective informs this new curriculum and influences the topics and resources selected for analysis. However, it is important to remember that the same curriculum is at pains to create a democratic terrain in the classroom in which all voices are recognized and respected. It is precisely the introduction of a multitude of conflicting perspectives that makes such a democratic inquiry possible.

NOTES

Chapter 2: Debate, Discussion, and Writing

Source for quote: "History is, indeed, an argument without end." Pieter Geyl (http://csbs.csusb.edu/history/history306/history306quote2.htm, "Quotes on History" compiled by Robert Blackey.

Essays by August Meier and Clayborne Carson found in *Taking Sides: Clashing Views on Controversial Issues in American History, Volume II Reconstruction to the Present (4th edition)*, Issue 16: "Was Martin Luther King, Jr.'s Leadership Essential to the Success of the Civil Rights Movement?", ed. Larry Madras and James M. SoRelle, (The Dushkin Publishing Group, Inc., 1991).

Chapter 3: Teaching Columbus

"What Was the Truth About the Spanish Conquest" was originally published in Madrid, 1864. A translation is available from James Lockhart and Enrique Otte, eds.,*Letters and People of the Spanish Indies: Sixteenth Century* (Cambridge University Press, 1976), pp. 220-222, 236, 239.

Chapter 5: Assignments and Activities: Developing Inquiry Skills

Newspaper sources used include: "Columbus Parade on the March," by Maurice Carroll, *New York Newsday,* October 9, 1990, p.19.

Photo with caption: "In Salvador, Indians Declare Columbus Day a Day of Mourning," Reuters, *The New York Times,* October 13, 1989, p. 8.

Two reviews of Kirkpatrick Sale's book on Columbus, *The Conquest of Paradise* are: "Uncovering the Discoverer," by Lawrence Hall (published in *The Newark Star Ledger,* January 4, 1991) and "Debunking Columbus," by historian William McNeil (published in *The New York Times Book Review* on October 7, 1990).

Basil Davidson's article, "Columbus: the bones and blood of racism" was published in *Race & Class*, 33, 3, (1992), p. 17.

Picture Credits

Page 26: Various portraits of Columbus (Chapter 4, p. 21) from *Columbus: His Enterprise,* by Hans Koning (Monthly Review Press, New York) 1976. page 21

Page 37: Spaniards hanging Indians and setting fire to their houses. from *Columbus: His Enterprise,* by Hans Koning (Monthly Review Press, New York) 1976. page 88

Page 49: Olmec stones heads (Chapter 5, p. 43) from *They Came Before Columbus,* by Ivan Van Sertima (Random House, New York) 1976. plates 29-30

Page 54: Picture of Columbus from *The Voyages of Christopher Columbus,* by Armstrong Perry (Random House, New York) 1950. p. 11